AUG 2 2 2007

DATE DUE

WEEKLY WR READER
EARLY LEARNING LIBRARY

This Is My Story

I Come from **Afghanistan**

by Valerie J. Weber

Reading consultant: Susan Nations, M.Ed., author/literacy coach/
consultant in literacy development

Please visit our web site at: www.garethstevens.com
For a free color catalog describing Weekly Reader® Early Learning Library's list
of high-quality books, call 1-877-445-5824 (USA) or 1-800-387-3178 (Canada).
Weekly Reader® Early Learning Library's fax: (414) 336-0164.

Library of Congress Cataloging-in-Publication Data

Weber, Valerie.
  I come from Afghanistan / by Valerie J. Weber.
    p. cm. — (This is my story)
  Includes bibliographical references and index.
  ISBN-10: 0-8368-7233-9 —ISBN-13: 978-0-8368-7233-0 (lib. bdg.)
  ISBN-10: 0-8368-7240-1 —ISBN-13: 978-0-8368-7240-8 (softcover)
    1. Afghan Americans—Social life and customs—Juvenile literature. 2. Immigrant children—United States—
Juvenile literature. 3. Immigrants—United States—Juvenile literature. 4. Mazar-e Sharif (Afghanistan)—
Social life and customs—Juvenile literature. 5. Afghanistan—Social life and customs—Juvenile literature.
6. United States—Social life and customs—Juvenile literature. I. Title.
  E184.A23W43 2007
  973'.0491593—dc22   2006018119

This edition first published in 2007 by
Weekly Reader® Early Learning Library
A Member of the WRC Media Family of Companies
330 West Olive Street, Suite 100
Milwaukee, WI 53212 USA

Art direction: Tammy West
Cover design, page layout, and maps: Charlie Dahl

Photography: All photos © Michael Jarrett Studio

Printed in the United States of America

1 2 3 4 5 6 7 8 9 10 09 08 07 06

Table of Contents

Cover and title page: I had fun eating cotton candy at the spring fair!

From Afghanistan to the United States

My name is Bahishta (bah-HEE-shtah). When I was two months old, I moved from a country called Afghanistan to the United States. Now I am nine years old.

I have been back to visit Afghanistan twice already. Next month, we are flying home to visit again.

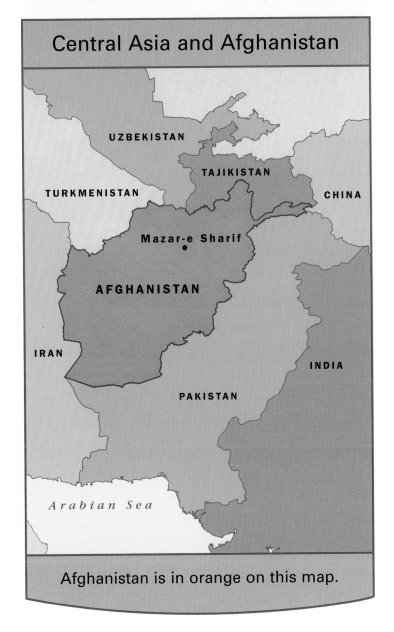

Central Asia and Afghanistan

UZBEKISTAN

TAJIKISTAN

TURKMENISTAN

CHINA

Mazar-e Sharif

AFGHANISTAN

IRAN

INDIA

PAKISTAN

Arabian Sea

Afghanistan is in orange on this map.

Afghanistan lies in Central Asia. It is about the size of Texas and has many huge mountains. We lived in a big, busy city in the north called Mazar-e Sharif. Farmlands surround the city.

Here is my sister Frishta, my dad, my mom, and me!

There have been many wars in my **homeland**. My father moved from Afghanistan to the United States because of one war. When he came back from the United States to visit his family, he met my mom. They got married. Because of another war, they decided to move back to the United States.

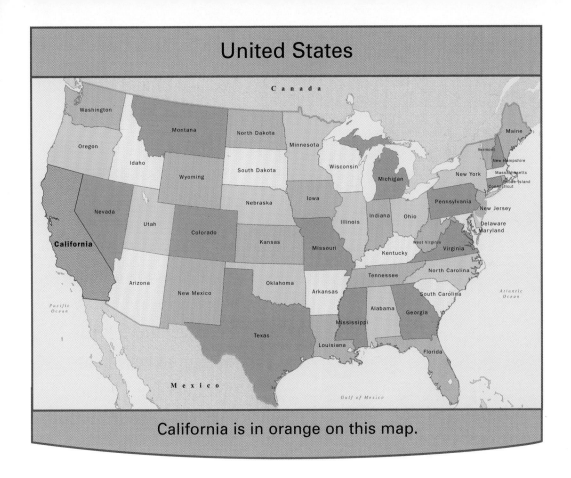

United States

California is in orange on this map.

My parents moved to southern California. Like Afghanistan, California has huge mountains. Southern California is a lot warmer than Afghanistan, though! It snows only in the mountains here. In Afghanistan, winter can last four months and bring heavy snows.

7

Life in Our House

We live in a house with wood floors and carpets. In Afghanistan, people usually sit on beautiful rugs on a dirt floor.

My uncle also lives with us. He keeps **homing pigeons** in the backyard. He races these birds. We can always hear them cooing. I also have canaries for pets.

Sometimes, I like to just sit on the steps of our house and think.

My sister Frishta and I have our own bedrooms, but we like to sleep together. Frishta is seven years old.

When we visit Afghanistan, we sometimes stay at my aunt's house. Then I sleep with four other people in my room! It is so much fun!

My sister is one of my best friends.

I hope these eggs turned out okay!

My mom is teaching me how to cook. I like American pizza and cheesecake, but I really love **Afghan** food. My favorite foods from Afghanistan are *mantu* and kabobs. Mantu is a kind of noodle stuffed with meat and covered with sauce. Kabobs are chunks of lamb or chicken pushed onto a **skewer** and grilled.

I also have to do chores at home. My sister and I take turns doing the dishes at night.

In northern Afghanistan, many girls go to school. In southern Afghanistan, girls are often kept home to do chores all day instead. The government wants all families to send both their boys and girls to school, however.

I would rather cook than do dishes!

Faith and Fun

Like most people in Afghanistan, we are **Muslims**. We follow the religion of **Islam**. In California, we go to the **mosque** every day after school. At the mosque, we learn about Islam, and we pray.

I am holding the **Koran**, the holy book of Islam.

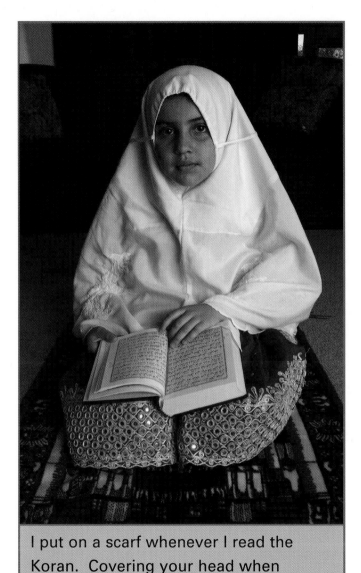

I put on a scarf whenever I read the Koran. Covering your head when reading the Koran is a sign of respect.

The Koran tells us what God wants from the Muslim people. We try to follow what the Koran says to do. It is written in a language called Arabic. I have been reading the Koran for two years.

There are thirty-four provinces in Afghanistan.

At home, I have a rug that shows all the **provinces** of Afghanistan. The names of the provinces are written in Arabic **characters**. We use Arabic when writing in Dari, one of the main languages of Afghanistan. My family also speaks Dari at home.

From left to right are my friend Tamanna, my sister Frishta, my friend Henna, and me.

Frishta, my friends, and I dress in our **traditional** clothes from Afghanistan sometimes. At holidays and special events, Afghan women and girls wear brightly colored dresses over pants. People from different parts of Afghanistan decorate their clothes differently. They use different patterns of beads and threads.

Sometimes we dance in our traditional clothes. Many people in Afghanistan love to dance. Our national dance is the *attan*. Big groups of men dance the attan to the beat of a drum. The drumbeat goes faster and faster, while the men **whirl**.

We like to make up our own dances.

I like hanging upside down at the park near my school.

In Afghanistan, I play many of the same games that kids play here. We jump rope, play hopscotch, and throw a ball. I play hide-and-seek and tag with my cousins when I visit Afghanistan.

My family invited my friends to join us at a Noruz festival in southern California.

A Spring Festival

Every year, people from Afghanistan celebrate Noruz at the beginning of spring. Noruz is a **festival** that marks the beginning of the New Year in Afghanistan. In the past, Afghans used a different calendar than many other people. On weekends during Noruz, kids can go on rides at fairgrounds and eat special foods.

There was lots of Afghan food at the festival. I loved the chicken kabobs and pita bread. They were almost as good as the kabobs in Afghanistan!

We started with kabobs. Later on, we went for the ice cream and cotton candy!

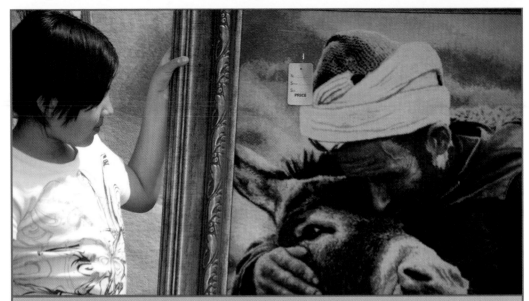

In Afghanistan, men sometimes wear **turbans** like the one on the man in this painting.

At the fair, I saw a painting of an Afghan farmer with his donkey. Most people farm or raise animals in Afghanistan. Much of the land is very rocky and dry or high in the mountains. It is hard to grow enough food to eat and to sell.

The fair reminded me of my family in Afghanistan. I miss my grandma, my grandpa, and my aunt and her kids. They live on a farm. I cannot wait to go back to visit!

I hope we get to dance in Afghanistan like I danced at the fair!

Glossary

Afghan — describes people, food, clothing, and customs from Afghanistan

characters — marks that stand for sounds or words

festival — a celebration of an event or special time

homeland — the country where someone comes from

homing pigeons — birds trained to fly quickly back to their homes when released far away

Islam — a religion in which followers believe in Allah, or God

Koran — a book of religious writings that Muslims believe were inspired by Allah, or God

mosque — a building that Muslims worship in

Muslims — people who believe in the religion of Islam

provinces — divisions of a country

skewer — a long thin metal or wooden stick used for cooking meat, fish, or vegetables on a grill

traditional — based on custom or an older fashion

turbans — head coverings made of a long cloth wrapped around a person's head or cap

whirl — to turn quickly in a circle

For More Information

Books

Afghanistan. Countries: Faces and Places (series). Kathryn Stevens (Child's World)

Afghanistan. Fact Finders (series). Gillia M. Olson (Capstone Press)

Afghanistan. Many Cultures, One World (series). Barbara Knox (Blue Earth Books)

The Man With Bad Manners. Idries Shah (Hoopoe Books)

Web Sites

Afghanistan for Kids
www.public.asu.edu/~apnilsen/afghanistan4kids/index2.html
Find games, stories, and information about Afghanistan

Growing Up in Afghanistan
library.thinkquest.org/CR0212462
An interactive site put together by students

Publisher's note to educators and parents: Our editors have carefully reviewed these Web sites to ensure that they are suitable for children. Many Web sites change frequently, however, and we cannot guarantee that a site's future contents will continue to meet our high standards of quality and educational value. Be advised that children should be closely supervised whenever they access the Internet.

Index

About the Author

Valerie Weber lives in Milwaukee, Wisconsin, with her husband and two daughters. She has been writing for children and adults for more than twenty-five years. She is grateful to both her family and friends for their support over that time. She would also like to thank the families who allowed her a glimpse of their lives for this series.